CUISINE FOR CATS

CUISINE FOR CATS

by

RICHARD GRAHAM

Illustrations by
DON GRANT

Pedigree Books
London

© Richard Graham 1980

Graham, Richard
    Cuisine for cats
    1. Cats – Food
    I. Title
    636′8′08′4   SF447.6

ISBN 0 905150 18 X

First published in Great Britain
by
Jay Landesman Limited
London W1

Third Edition April 1985
Fourth Edition August 1985
Pedigree Books
23 Wandsworth Bridge Road
London SW6

Printed and bound in Great Britain by
Anchor Brendon Ltd, Tiptree, Essex

CONTENTS

For ANYA

con amore

Many of the world's great cookery writers have at some time told us how they first came to take an interest in their craft. Robert Carrier fell in love with the odours emerging from the kitchen of his grandmother's summer home on Cape Cod when the family came home from church on Sunday mornings. Elizabeth David lost her child's heart to a set of miniature copper pans given to her on her fourth birthday. The immortal Escoffier was moved by the need to earn a living as soon as he left school. *

In my own case the start came later. A week or two after marriage to be precise, and the catalyst was a small Abyssinian cat of six weeks who bore the professional name of Rifan Sabishi and was among our wedding presents.

My wife was a ballet dancer, and therefore on most days of the week she spent her evenings in the theatre, while I stayed at home to look after the cat. Because it was such a very small cat, there seemed no point to my specially cooking it miniscule meals of the kind deemed suitable for cats, and so I cooked one dish for us both and gave it a portion of this.

The cat approved of the arrangement — a favourite meal of hers was a mixed grill with a saucer of dry vin rosé — and I became absorbed in its culinary likes and dislikes and began to experiment along the lines dictated by them.

It led, however, to repercussions which continued through several generations of cats and for all I know may persist to this day among their descendants. For Rifan Sabishi made a young marriage, meeting her husband rather unromantically in a cattery at a place called Wickford in Essex — not an area in which I myself would choose to honeymoon — and after a very short courtship presented him with a young family.

8   As soon as the time came for her to wean her off-

spring, she took them aside and told them firmly what and what not to eat: all tinned catfoods were out; fish in, but only if fresh and not frozen; all offal was totally banned from their regime, and if any kitten attempted to breakfast off devilled kidneys or lunch off *fegato veneziano*, it got a cuff on the head that discouraged this practice for the rest of its life. The creatures were the despair of every catfood manufacturer in the country.

Whether it was their mother's table training or mine that made them so fastidious I don't know, but they were all tarred with the same brush and kept it up throughout their lives. Some of them, of course, had to go out into the world to earn their livings, and in one or two cases we lost touch. But in others not, one of these being a lady in north London who purchased one of the brood and rang up almost daily to enquire about medication and food. She had a very squeaky, singsong voice and when she first rang, I thought she was a Chinese child and said so. My wife was constantly going over, between ballet performances, to north London, like an unpaid veterinary surgeon, and came back to say that the cat was just as selective about its diet as when it had lived with us.

Sabishi had been named after a Japanese word in one of Han Suyin's books, but when a Japanese scholar explained that this did not quite mean what my wife thought it did, an indignant cat contracted it to Sabi. In adopting the -i suffix, she was a pioneer, for the current vogue of changing old-fashioned girls' names like Antonia, Jacqueline and Martha to Toni, Jacki and Marti had not yet come in. The other name change we had was Araminta, who having been christened this, was told by the feline equivalent of the Kennel Club that another cat already possessed it. It seemed that in the rarified world of Abyssinian cats, two animals cannot have the same name; it was rather like a small-part actor registering himself as Laurence Olivier and then coming up against the might of Equity.

I thought for a while, and then bestowed on the cat the name of Terraminta, who was a character in one of Dryden's seventeenth-century tragedies. It was not sufficiently different from Araminta and she did not turn round and start calling herself Terri.

While all this was going on, Sabi produced more children. Multiple births are quite frequent in the cat world, but the rate at which Sabi had them would have been more appropriate to the prototype Irish Catholic mother in the Bogside area of Londonderry. I regret to say, however, that there the analogy ends, for piety did not come into it, and the father of these infant cats was not that of their elder half-brothers and sisters.

I am sure the reader will understand that I am not a narrow-minded person, but it is my contention that if our pets are to share fully in the life of the human household, including its gastronomic pleasures, they must conform to the decent norms of the society in which we live, and which exclude polygamy. In writing my cookery books for domestic pets, my aim is to give them a grounding in domestic science and cooking, and through this noble art to elevate their minds to a greater knowledge and understanding of the human condition. Morals, ethics and religion are all a part of this, and I am already sketching out my ideas for a continuation of this series with books on all three.

Until they are published, your cat has to remain in ignorance of the doctrine of original sin, and I can only hope that through setting it a thrice-daily example at your table, you will lay in it the foundations of a love which passes all understanding.

An instance of my personal experience which I should like to quote is that of Benedict, Terraminta's somewhat corpulent half-brother, gourmand rather than gourmet, and the Billy Bunter of the tribe. My wife was lying in bed with influenza in our little Chelsea house, and I was sitting on it making suitable noises of sympathy, when in came Benedict, carrying a small bunch of hothouse grapes in his mouth, and jumped up on the bed covers to deposit them in front of my wife, just as I might have done had I any money. However, it transpired that Benedict had none either and had not been out to the fruiterers in the King's Road. but had in some mystical fashion cottoned on to the fact that the etiquette of sick-visiting calls for the presentation of grapes. He had in fact collected them from the sideboard in the dining-room and without prompting carried them up two flights of stairs.

But then you may remember the tale of Dr Johnson's famous cat, who appeared in the dining-room at Crown Court one day with two mice it had caught and put one of them on Dr Johnson's place and one on its own at the other end of the table. The moral is simple. If you look after your cat, it will look after you.

This includes not giving it canned food. You may have watched some pampered and highly-salaried cat gobbling 'Yummy' on the television and thought how good it must be. Probably that cat has had no breakfast before setting out for the television studio and by the time its commercial comes on would eat anything set before it. But how do you know that what it is eating is not caviar rather than 'Yummy'?

I speak with some authority on this, for at one time. in addition to performing ballet, my wife participated in many of these television advertisements, and some of the substances used bore no resemblance to the ones being advertised. Don't let your cat be the victim of a con trick. It won't thank you for it.

R.G.

---

* This is the author's version of these writers' beginnings, not theirs — Editor.

SOUP OF THE DAY

Like the late Duke of Windsor, I used to be a great adherent of British Rail's train ferry service to Paris, arguing that if it was good enough for the Duke, it was good enough for me, and perhaps subconsciously hoping that if there were not enough single compartments to go round, he might have to share a double one with me.

One of the charms of the service was that on leaving Victoria you could get an excellent à la carte supper in a restaurant car with comfortable chairs and plenty of leg room. One evening, as I was sitting there, I overheard the conversation between the man at the table across the gangway and the attendant. The man was studying the menu card.

"What's the soup du jour?" he asked.

"That's soup du jour, sir," the attendant replied.

"Yes, but what is it?"

"Soup du jour, sir."

"Yes, but what is it today?" asked the man, putting

WAITER! THERE'S A WHITE LONGHAIR IN MY SOUP

the stress on the last word.

"Soup du jour, sir," said the attendant, scratching his head in puzzlement. "Same as what it always is. That's a kind of brown Windsor soup," he explained.

Perhaps they laid it on specially for HRH. I don't know. But I always give my cat the same soup, day after day, only it is a fish soup, for cats, and we too like these little continental touches like calling it soup du jour.

It is not difficult to make. You need first to prepare a fish stock, and for this I use either a cod's head, if I can get one, or the skeletons of Dover sole which Bill, my fishmonger, gives me when he has finished filleting them; chop a large onion, a carrot and a stick of celery, or substitute dried celery flakes if you have no fresh celery in the house. A bay leaf, a bouquet garni, some parsley stalks, crushed black peppercorns and a glass of dry white wine if you have any open. Put them all in a pan and simmer for about 45 minutes before you strain off the liquid.

This will give you about a quart of stock, or will if you added two pints of water in the first place, something I forgot to tell you to do. Otherwise you will have a burnt pan and a horrible mess to clean up. Into this add a 397 gram tin of tomatoes — they now come in this size to prove the ease and beauty of metrication — with ¾lb of white fish, and simmer for 30 minutes. You can if you wish add a little powdered saffron to colour it, but first read my note in the glossary on the price of this.

Lastly, put the soup through a sieve or liquidiser, but first remove any bones as liquidised fish bones are not particularly appetising and if not broken down completely may stick in your cat's throat.

As to what fish should be used, any non-oily white fish is suitable. Conger eel is excellent, so is cod or whiting, also rock salmon, which I tell the cat is dog-fish and the dog catfish. Again see the glossary of terms.

In the days before frozen and convenience foods, a cat used to regard a cod's head as a great delicacy, and during the grim economic depression of the early 1930s, considered itself extremely lucky to get its paws on one.

In many a north-east fishing port, where rows of laid-up trawlers lay rusting at anchor year after year, a cat would wait all day, in freezing weather conditions, for a ship to land its catch, and then, as those fisher-lassies gutted and prepared the glittering harvest of the sea for market, the cat would pounce on the morsels that fell from their knife blades onto the oily cobbles of the quayside.

Of course, not every out-of-work cat got a whole cod's head to itself, but the animal fortunate enough to do so would withdraw with it into the lee of the icy wind and make a very satisfactory meal of its haul before retreating into the drab side streets and the back-to-back dwelling where it lived.

Sometimes it had to make do with a piece of cod's roe. Taramasalata we call it today, but there were no Greek island holidays then for the cats of Hull and Grimsby, or their masters, and they wouldn't have known what you were talking about if you had mentioned the word in the harsh epoch of which I am writing.

And if they had, where were they to get olive oil and garlic? Cats had no money for luxuries in those days, and there were no electric liquidisers either. But sometimes, if the roe fell in the grooves of a dockside rail track, the wheels of a passing train would pound it to the correct consistency of taramasalata, though the cat, brought up in a more homely Northern dialect, would think of the stuff as mashed cod's roe.

It is as much of a myth that the Isle of Man's famous kippers are born without tails as that whitings suck their tails as they swim about in the sea. But it is said that a good Manxman always docks the appendage with a sharp knife before serving the fish to his cat, in order to prevent it having feelings of envy towards its kippered relation.

This is, of course, hearsay on my part, as I have never been to the Isle of Man, and at present am having difficulty in finding a Manx kipper to try out on my cat. Even when I do, I shall have more difficulty in finding the money for it, because as I was saying to Bill, my fishmonger, only the other morning, I do consider ten shillings (or one dollar) exorbitant for a breakfast kipper.

Bill agreed with me, and told me that in his young days in the fish trade, presumably not long before the 1939 war, he used to sell the things at one old halfpenny per pair. The present-day price represents an inflationary factor of 24,000%, or if I may put it in words twenty-four thousand per cent.

However, I'd rather pay it than have my cat eat the 'boil-in-the-bag' kippers that appear in the freezer cabinets of supermarkets, and the reason I look for Manx kippers is that they are only subjected to natural methods of curing. A kipper should be pale in colour, not mahogany brown, which means it has been artificially dyed. And it should be a smallish fish, unlike so many of the monsters on sale today, because otherwise the kippering process (which is essentially smoking the raw fish over an oak fire), does not penetrate right through the delicate flesh.

And another thing. I don't like them poached in water, as many people do, because this removes 50% of the flavour and food value. I grill them under medium heat; fierce heat destroys the flavour and too

18

little heat dries out the natural oils.

Usually I eat them in bed with the cat at breakfast time. It is particularly fond of the backbone that buckles up with the heat of the cooking, leaving a bit of skin adhering to it. I content myself with the rest and give the cat the skin when I've finished.

REMEMBRANCE SUNDAY
or
GRILLED FISH PIE

The usual technique for making a fish pie is to cook it in a hot oven, but I may be the world's only chef to have invented a grilled one.

I had invited some people to Sunday luncheon, and knowing that one of them shared my cat's fondness for fish pie, prepared one of these before settling down to the Sunday papers. All I would have to do later would be put it in the oven for half an hour and bring it to the table.

In due course the guests arrived. I gave them each a Pimm's, and after a little polite conversation moved to the oven. I pressed the automatic ignition device and was rewarded by the sound as of a cigarette lighter being clicked at frequent intervals by an invisible gasman. But the oven did not light, and after ten minutes' clicking still did not light. It had always lit previously, indeed only a few days before had done so with such explosive force that it had set me on fire and destroyed the remaining hair on my frontal lobes. I had spent a fortune on having a new ignition device fitted to the stove, and now it was refusing to work at all.

The female guests advised me not to get agitated and to come and have another drink before I tried again. Afterwards I held a now sore thumb on the 19 ignition button for a further ten minutes, without any result.

How were we going to cook the fish pie? The cat, I knew, liked raw fish but not my guests. One of them suggested putting it in a bain marie, but I said that it was a very large fish pie, intended for more guests than had actually turned up, and that heating it through by this method would take several hours.

The guests suggested mary-bathing only as much of the fish pie as was currently needed. I objected on aesthetic grounds. It was a very handsome fish pie, and I wasn't going to have it cut up in bits, not before it arrived on the table anyway.

A French woman guest — the French are a practical nation — suggested that we put it under the grill. I maintained that what would result would be a burnt top and a raw interior. Eventually we compromised by covering it with aluminium foil. Two Pimms later we tested it. The foil was preventing the heat from reaching the plate.

The French lady got a sharp knife and introduced a series of vents in it. This did the trick, because by tea-time the dish was quite warm though not noticeably cooked.

The French lady ate her share of it hurriedly and departed, already late for a ceremony she had to attend with her diplomat husband. For it was Remembrance Sunday, and one I shall never forget, but if you have an oven that lights and want to try the dish, I thoroughly recommend the following recipe.

Fry an onion and a chopped stick of celery (or celery flakes) in butter, adding two tablespoons of flour to make a roux. Add ¾ pint of milk gradually until you have a smooth white sauce, then stir in a tablespoonful of Worcester sauce and half as much anchovy essence, a little thyme, salt, pepper and chopped parsley. In the meantime, cut up 1½lbs white fish — haddock for preference, or cod or coley — and with ¼lb sliced mushrooms put it in the bottom of a casserole and top the mixture with two sliced hard-boiled eggs and a handful of cooked prawns before pouring the sauce over. Sprinkle with grated Parmesan cheese, top with a thin layer of puréed potato and cook in the oven at 375° for 30 minutes.

This quantity should feed six people or three large cats.

 STUFFED CARP or MUDDY WATERS

Recently I had some minor disagreements with my publisher, mainly over the kind of fish cats prefer, and nobbling him in his quaint Soho office, which is a kind of Anglo-American cross between Charles Dickens and The Great Gatsby, I let forth.

"Look, Jay," I said, "I don't want to carp but . . ."

"*You* don't want a carp," he shouted, "*You* don't want a carp. What's wrong with a carp? It's a fine fish. Put it in the book," he added with finality.

"Look, Jay," I said, "All I was trying to say . . ."

"You always knock down my good ideas. Put it in the book. It's a great idea."

The next thing was to get hold of a carp. I tried ringing up a few monasteries to see if the monks still breed them for Lent and fast-days. They don't.

I had an idea that they are the sort of fish that retired gas board officials catch on the banks of disused canals, but the idea of wandering along the banks of the Grand Union Canal near Brentford Gasworks trying to persuade one of them to sell me his catch somehow didn't appeal to me.

I finally set off for a suburban emporium in Enfield where they sell fish to fish fanciers. They had carp, in a variety of ornamental colours, but one large enough to make a meal for the cat would have been too expensive. I could have had a very large and handsome

21

salmon, or even lobster in a smart restaurant for the same price.

Besides, I thought, carp are alleged to taste of mud, and apparently the only way to get rid of this is to keep them alive in fresh water for some days before killing and cooking them. I have the choice here of the kitchen sink or the bath: the cat would be up on the draining board the moment my back was turned and have the fish out of the water in no time, displaying all the dexterity and expertise of a retired gas board official; my bath is a sunken job and access to it all too easy for a cat.

 FRITTO MISTO DI MARE

Only last Easter I was given halibut for dinner, purchased under the mistaken impression that it had been caught the day before off the shores of North Wales and landed at a little fish-dock near Bangor. A closer look at the wrappings, however, revealed that the supposedly local-caught fish had been hooked off Greenland by a Japanese fishing vessel or possibly off Japan by a Greenland one.

This kind of thing will increase as the century moves on. Already it is reported that the English consumer's taste in fish has been so widened by Mediterranean holidays that it cannot be met from the catches in home waters.

Yet Billingsgate Market is about to be demolished. The deep-sea fishing industry of Hull and Grimsby is but a wraith of its former self, while other ports have packed it in altogether. The fisher-lassies of Great Yarmouth have passed into mythology, and there are but 2,000 fish shops in Britain as against 12,000 thirty-five years ago.

Dublin Bay prawns, otherwise known as scampi, do

FLYING TONIGHT

DonGrant

not come from Dublin Bay, but from Malaya, Indonesia or Bangladesh. Already besugo, lithrini, bonito, wong fish, tilapia and trevalli have reached our shores, but not by swimming here. And worse still, we are not only to have these exotics foisted upon us, but South African fish which is processed, laminated and layered like plywood, which no doubt it will resemble in taste as well as texture.

Of course, the handyman can may find it useful for doing jobs about the house, but the older generation of cat, reared before the advent of fish fingers, is muttering darkly as it peers into the dish containing its evening meal. It does not want junk food of this kind, cod in parsley sauce and so on, boiled in a transparent plastic bag.

I think perhaps I should have called this recipe 'A Pretty Kettle of Fish' instead of giving it some fancy foreign name like fritto misto di mare.

It came as a shock to me recently to learn that a cat about to enter hospital for a minor operation is allowed no breakfast. But it came as even more of a shock to the cat. Normally it sits on the bed beside my breakfast tray, sharing whatever cooked dish I have prepared for myself and washing it down with a saucer of milky tea.

But on this particular morning it was going to be out of luck, and I thought of all my favourite breakfast dishes which I should enjoy not having to share: kedgeree, devilled kidneys, poached finnan haddock, grilled trout with bacon. In the end I plumped for the trout with bacon; it is not difficult to prepare and is something one doesn't see often these days.

I got up, put the trout on the grill, while I squeezed some oranges and put the kettle on for tea before turning the fish and adding three rashers of best back bacon. I laid the tray with my favourite Royal Worcester blue dragon china, and when all was ready, carried it upstairs and got back into bed.

The cat purred loudly until it noticed that there was only one plate instead of two. I tried to explain about anaesthetics, while the cat decided to use persuasion rather than force, butting its head against the hand in which I was holding a fish fork and making the noises traditional to a hungry cat. In doing so, it somehow knocked over my cup of tea and, scalded by this, leapt on to my chest, scattering more very hot tea over myself and causing the tray to fall, first sideways, and then onto the floor.

Before I could recover myself, the cat had jumped down and removed the trout, with two of the rashers of bacon, to an inaccessible position under the bed from which I could not dislodge it.

It is one thing to pride oneself on having floors clean enough to eat off, but quite another to have one's

25

trout with bacon eaten off them by a cat who has been forbidden all nourishment. The upshot was that I had to ring the vet and call off the operation, much to the relief of the cat, who was now purring happily and had forgotten all about the hot tea.

I would suggest firmly locking your cat out of your bedroom before you start breakfasting on grilled trout and bacon. Just cook it in the usual way, put it on a heated plate, avoid all contact with cats and don't come out of your room until you have finished every scrap.

 ## LOBSTER TEAS FOR CATS

The year we took our cat on holiday to Cornwall, we chose Mousehole, which, as the reader may know, is a famous fishing village on the cliffs beyond Penzance and about the last there is before you get to Land's End.

It was not a success. The train journey from London is a long one, and by the time we arrived in Penzance the animal was tired and fractious. So was I, the guard having made me pay the same fare for the cat as I would have done had it been a thirteen year old child weighing nearly a hundredweight. Had its basket been full of picnic, or even dead cat, there would have been no charge, but because the creature was alive, though barely so by the end of the trip, I had to pay British Rail a king's ransom.

The atmosphere grew worse. The taxi-driver I asked at the station to take us to Mousehole said it was pronounced 'Muzzle' which did not go down at all well with the cat. As the days went by, it showed only too plainly that it felt cheated. We stayed in a rented caravan, which in the nature of things has no wainscoating and therefore no mouseholes, whereas the cat had assumed that the place was a kind of feline equivalent of the Yorkshire grouse moors in August.

In the end we went back into Penzance, had a lobster tea and caught the train home. But this time, I introduced a couple of strong sleeping pills into the cat's portion of lobster and put her basket on the luggage rack covered by a coat so that I didn't have to pay a child's fare for one small cat.

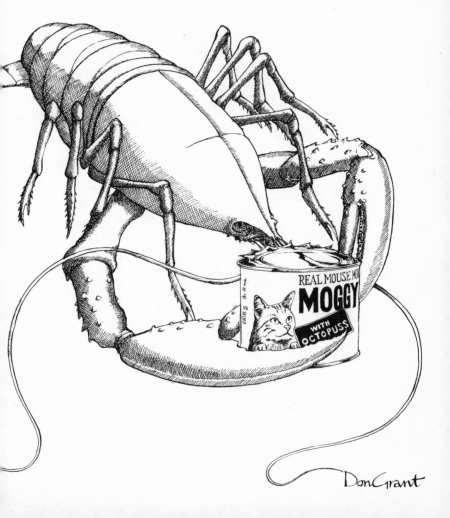

Portofino, for those who don't already know it, is a charming and picturesque little resort on the Italian Riviera. But the feeding of its resident cats is a matter of indifference to the inhabitants.

When we stayed there for a holiday some years ago, my wife tried to remedy the situation by doling out portions of her own meals to them, and the cats of Portofino, unaccustomed to such delicacies as fillet steak and goujons of sole, clustered round our water-front table. The maître d'hotel was not pleased by this conduct and asked her to stop it. She looked up at him with startled innocence and asked why.

The man waved his hands high in the air and, launching into the English multiplication table with great dexterity, replied: "Signora, now you 'ave two cats. You feed 'em da food. Then you 'ave four cats. Then eight cats, seexteen cats, thair-tee two cats, seexty-four cats. *Boom*. Soon Portofino all cats, no more people," he concluded with finality.

Of course, my wife merely moved to another table and continued to feed the cats from there as surreptitiously as she could.

I have not been back to Portofino since, so I do not know if the maître d'hotel's prediction came true. Perhaps it did, and this was the reason Mr Rex Harrison sold that nice villa of his and moved away.

BIRDS OF A FEATHER

Anyone who has been to Florence will have noticed delectable restaurants festooned outside with strings of small dead birds, looking for all the world as if they had been hunted down by the local cats and sold by them to the restaurant owners as an extra source of income, undeclared for tax.

But in fact it is the human race which is responsible and not the Florentine cat, the unfortunate creatures being snared by methods inimical to the British sporting instinct, which is further exacerbated by their smallness.

For while it is one thing to eat a well-hung partridge or grouse at a table laden with decent family silver, it is quite another to sit gobbling a brochette of thrushes or larks with their heads still *in situ*, and most Anglo-Italian cookery books steer well clear of the whole distasteful subject.

However, supposing that your own cat, here in Britain, has committed the dastardly act of nobbling some friendly bird in the garden, and has hopefully dragged it into the kitchen, for you first to admire and then cook? You will, of course, give it a homily on the evils of its nature, possibly administering a physical beating at the same time. This can only puzzle the cat, who has enviously observed you at other times potting away with a 12-bore gun at other birds with much more

DonGrant

beautiful plumage than the little specimen it has just bagged.

But you have made your point to the cat, and the next thing is to dispose of the corpse. If you bury it in the garden, the cat will only watch where you have put it and dig it up again as soon as your back is turned; the waste disposal grinder is too cruel; the dustbin callous, though cremation, if you have an open fire, is feasible.

But why waste food in a starving world? Do as the Italians do. Pluck the little bird, impale it on a skewer, brush it with olive oil, salt and pepper, add a bay leaf and a few mixed herbs, and roast it on the spit of your rotisserie.

I would not advise serving it on a bed of polentà, as the Florentine restaurateurs do, since cats prefer a starch-free diet, and this applies to serving it on triangles of fried bread as well. Just serve it up as it comes off the roasting spit. It will give the cat an appetite for hunting and save you having to buy it tins of Kit-e-Kat all the time.

I have always liked the character in one of Nancy Mitford's early novels who on a first visit to Rome ingenuously remarked that all the city's ancient ruins seemed to be named after London cinemas and theatres.

But the part of Rome known as the Largo di Torre Argentina hardly seems to qualify unless you can read into it some tenuous connection with the current West End stage presentation of the musical *Evita*, with its theme song of 'Don't Cry for Me, Argentina'. However, what the place lacks in theatricality is made up for by the presence of the eternal city's stray cats, who have established for themselves an animal sanctuary and hostel among the remains of these antique temples.

It is not perhaps run on quite the same lines as would be a well-endowed cats' home in England, but daily, at certain hours, there is an exodus of elderly English ladies from Babington's Tea Rooms beside the Spanish Steps in the direction of the Largo Argentina, where they feed and converse with the animals and generally obstruct the Rome municipality's efforts to have them — the cats — removed elsewhere.

I suppose that when I next go out there I shall have to pay a visit too, and I was wondering what to take in the way of food when I remembered that Miss Mitford's book was called *Pigeon Pie*.

Pigeon is eaten quite a lot in Italy, and done the way I like it, should be perfect fare for a hungry Roman cat.

Allow one pigeon per cat, getting your poulterer to split the birds lengthways. From the pigeon livers make a stuffing, finely chopping the liver up with butter, parsley, salt and pepper. Stuff the pigeon halves with this.

Now line a pie-dish with strips of puff pastry and

33

cover the bottom with small pieces of good stewing steak, allowing about 8 oz. per cat. Put the halved birds on top of the steak, insides upwards, and between them place sliced yolks of hard-boiled eggs. Season the dish and add a little grated nutmeg, followed by small pieces of unsalted butter scattered about the dish.

Some veal stock should also be added, but it is advisable to dissolve a little gelatine in it previously so that when cooked and cold it will form a jelly. Otherwise the juice, when you empty out the dish, may run into the ground before the cats have time to lick it up.

Now using the rest of your pastry, roll out a lid, using any surplus trimmings to decorate the top with cat motifs of your choice. Bake it in a middling oven for about 2½ hours, or longer if you have a large number of cats to feed and the pie is a big one.

When it is cool, take it down to the Largo Argentina and serve it through the railings, either wearing very stout gloves or using a long-handled instrument. These cats are of Latin temperament, and their table manners are different from ours.

CATVLLVS

A TASTE OF IRELAND

I have always been interested in the problem of animal boredom, and what ways and means there are of combating it.

An interesting experiment was carried out in the Germany of the Weimar Republic by a friend of mine. Although still only a child, she made a point of drawing pictures in coloured chalks on the undersides of the furniture in her family home in Dresden, realising that the cats spent a lot of their time crouched beneath it, and would otherwise not have much to look at.

Unfortunately she was unable to reach any conclusive findings, because in 1933 Hitler came to power, and while he appears not to have had much personally against cats, he had against my friend, who by then had taken up satirical cabaret as a profession, in company with Erika Mann, daughter of the famous German author Thomas Mann. Both young ladies had a taste and talent for making public mockery of their new leader, and as a consequence my friend had to leave Germany in a hurry, without cats or furniture, though if the latter wasn't fire-bombed in 1944 or subsequently dusted underneath by an over-conscientious German hausfrau, the pictures may still be *in situ*.

What with Hitler and the incorporation of Dresden into East Germany, my friend wasn't able to go back and find out. But her travels took her to many other places, including the Theatre Royal at Waterford in Ireland, a move which I engineered.

By this time she had become a United States citizen, and the Theatre Royal Waterford was one which in a century's history had never before seen a travelling theatrical company from the United States and was not to do so again until the entourage of the late John F. Kennedy reached the same neck of the woods a couple of years later.

Unlike President Kennedy's, however, our visit was not a triumph, German satirical cabaret not being understood in Waterford, and on one distinctly peculiar night, we had an audience of only 26 people, all of whom turned out to be local Waterford Protestants because, we discovered later, there was an unwritten convention in Waterford that Protestants attended the Theatre Royal on Tuesdays. They were there to give us, as strangers and therefore suspected Protestants, moral support.

After that nobody came for the rest of the week. I now realise that I should have invited the cats of Waterford to fill the rows of empty seats and see if the performance alleviated their boredom.

It would have been interesting to see their reactions, and then we could have taken them out to supper with the cast, though what they would have got at that hour of the night I just can't think, as in those days Waterford was mostly into high teas at around 6 p.m.

 TURKISH DELIGHT

A minor curiosity in the Ireland of my youth was a Turkish Delight manufactory and retail shop in the city of Cork. It was a curiosity because thirty years ago, with the exception of a very good French restaurant in Dublin, ethnic cooking had made no impact what-

soever on Ireland, and to find Mr Hadji Bey purveying his sweetmeats to the people of Cork seemed as out of place as it would be to find a Sweeney's Railway Bar and Select Lounge dispensing Guinness's Stout by the shores of the Bosphorus.

I often wondered if Mr Bey came from there, or perhaps from the shores of Lake Van in south-east Turkey, and if the latter whether he kept in his Cork home one or more of the breed of cat that takes its name from it. As cat fanciers know, nature has given the Van cat an extra layer of fur, which enables it to take to the waters of the lake for exercise and recreation, making it the only cats' lido in the world.

I have tried to get my own cat to take up swimming, but a ten foot square ornamental pond in a small Chelsea garden is not quite the same as Lake Van. Far from demonstrating an ability at the crawl, the animal displayed panic and consternation, and broke the stem of one of my best water lilies in its attempts to get back on to terra firma.

Feeling slightly ashamed of myself, I proffered it a piece of Mr Bey's Turkish Delight, which I still have despatched to me by post from Cork. The animal shook not only its head at me but its wet fur, spattering my new white trousers, and then savaged my right hand with its teeth. I don't think it has a sweet tooth.

On the way to the dry cleaners and the chemist, I passed my local Turkish takeaway. It is called Istanbul Express, and has one of those large lumps of coagulated meat revolving in the window. I didn't think that with a lacerated hand I should be able to cook that night, so I went in and ordered a large doner kebab, to be ready for me on my return from the chemists.

I ate it in the street, and gave the free piece of Turkish Delight to the cat when I got home.

I am Church of England, but when I was staying in Jerusalem, I had to conform to the dietary laws prevalent there. I managed to get out of what the King David Hotel's menu called 'Pancakes Made Like Momma Makes 'Em', but no way could I get butter served with my bacon at breakfast time.

When it came to fish, lobster was out too. I had to make do with a spiny beast dredged out of the Lake of Galilee and callked a St Peter's fish. It was deep-fried whole, head, spines, fins, the lot, and served with chips and Coca-Cola at an open-air café on the edge of the lake.

Somehow I didn't take terribly to deep-fried fish in the blazing sunshine of an Israeli summer afternoon, but I suppose that the cats of Israel have to keep to the rules just as I did. It is no use their asking for lobster if there isn't any, but if I were a cat and didn't like St Peter's fish, I think I would go for carp.

The reason I suggest this is that I have a book called *The Master Book of Fish*. It is dedicated to The Fishermen of England and contains over one thousand ways of preparing fish.

Four of them are for carp à la juive, the first being the straight version, the others à l'orientale, au persil (parsley, not the detergent) and aux raisins. Of course, these recipes are for orthodox cats, which you could hardly say about mine with its eccentric ways and fondness for lobster. But if it ever does bring home a nice Jewish tom-cat one day, I think I shall give the guest carp au persil, which avoids the horseradish sauce, strip almonds and scalded raisins of the other three recipes.

40

GASTRIC JEWS

DonGrant

OEUFS SUR PLAT

Somewhere in a back issue of *The Good Food Guide*, a publication which impertinently tries to rival mine, there is a reference to the resident parrot at the Blue Bell Inn at Llangurig, a place featured in my *Good Dog's Cook Book* under the guise of The Twelve Dogs.

What *The Good Food Guide* did not reveal is that the parrot, though purchased at the Top People's Store in Knightsbridge and brought up amid a mainly Welsh clientèle, spoke with a strong Cockney accent, and that although sold to its owner as a male, underwent a sex change at the age of seventeen and laid three eggs in the bar of the Twelve Dogs.

Mrs Stanton, affronted by this challenge to her bird's virility, immediately got into her car and came home with a dozen hens, followed by a hen-house on a lorry. Behind the hotel ran an extraordinary monument to human folly, a railway embankment that in the hundred and twenty years of its existence had seen but one train, on an unrecorded day of 1861.

It was still known as The Railway, and it was on the part owned by her that Mrs Stanton proposed to establish the latest of her enterprises. Comparatively few people have ever had to manhandle a large hen-house up the side of a Welsh railway embankment, and when we at last succeeded, exhausted, Mrs Stanton rewarded us by a free issue of smoked salmon to precede the hotel's set dinner.

As I ate mine, I had an idea and surreptitiously concealed a piece of the fish in a paper napkin which I slipped in a pocket. My target was Blodwen, the hotel's resident cat.

Around 2 a.m., when as usual the staff were refreshing themselves in the bar, I quietly made my way into the kitchen and started work. Into a mixing bowl I cracked the three parrot's eggs, and beat them up with salt, pepper and the chopped smoked salmon while I melted a little Welsh butter in a saucepan on top of the Aga before adding the egg and smoked salmon mixture to it with a dessertspoonful of double cream, stirring the lot gently over a low heat until it was of a smooth, creamy consistency and topping it with a dash of cayenne pepper.

There had never been much love lost between the parrot and Blodwen, who seemed thoroughly to enjoy eating the fruit of the parrot's loins, or wherever it is that young parrots come from, and I recommend your trying it out on your cat.

I find that the best time is when he or she has come in tired after a night on the tiles as we all do from time to time, and if you can't get parrots' eggs, use hens' ones, with perhaps a glass of champagne if you are feeling thirsty.

GINGER & PICKLES
or
HOW TO MAKE KEDGEREE

In the sixties we used to buy our cats' fish at a shop round the corner from us in Chelsea. It was called Ginger & Pickles, not officially, but by my wife, who was a keen student of Beatrix Potter and convinced that the two fishmongers resembled nothing so much as the characters in Miss Potter's book of that name.

Ginger was, if you remember, a yellow tom-cat, and Pickles a terrier, and the small general shop they ran together foundered through a lack of business acumen and their giving too much credit to their

43

customers. Today we should probably call it lack of cash flow, for when the rates demand came in and there was no money to meet them, the business collapsed completely and was the victim of a take-over bid by a hen called Sally Henny Penny.

Indeed, although I do not think that Miss Potter intended it, a parallel could be drawn between this situation and that of many present-day businesses in the King's Road, near which Ginger and Pickles conduct their trade in fish to this day. But by giving close attention to their customers, and not much credit, they have managed to survive the economic storm that has hit so many traders in the wet fish business and meet with equanimity the Royal Borough of Kensington & Chelsea's exorbitant demands for rates.

Ginger is on his own now, for Pickles retired some while ago, not to become a gamekeeper as his namesake did on becoming redundant but, in keeping with the spirit of the times, to take a university course in business management.

I see Ginger in the shop most days, and am hoping that when this book is published, he can be persuaded to stock copies of it on the shelf next to the golden breadcrumbs where they will not get spattered by wet fish.

On the basis of you-scratch-my-back-and-I'll-scratch-yours, I shall in return buy from Ginger a smoked haddock, and hope that he won't remember that that was all the yellow tom-cat in the book ever got to eat. For since they had no money, the two shopkeepers had to eat the stocks of food in the shop. Pickles got the biscuits and Ginger the haddock.

I shall use mine to make a kedgeree. Gently poach the haddock in equal parts of milk and water and then skin and de-bone it. In an ounce of butter fry a chopped onion until it is soft and golden and then into an ovenproof serving dish put eight ounces of cooked long-grained rice, two ounces of melted butter, the cooked onion, two ounces of seedless raisins which have

44

previously been soaked in warm water, the chopped whites of two hard-boiled eggs, seasoning and the flaked fish. Mix them together and warm through in a low oven, then grate the cooked egg yolks over the top and scatter it with chopped parsley.

I usually serve it with mango chutney, but when I tried it with a little ground ginger and some pickles that I had to hand, it tasted equally delicious.

OEUFS FLORENTINE

All the cats I have known have liked their food. On the other hand there are people who don't. They can be divided into the "I can't be bothered" and the "I don't think food's all that important" factions. The latter mean "I don't find food important when you think of all those works of art in the Uffizi waiting to be seen and we've so little time in this life to do it".

Cats are different. A cat will take infinite pains to track down a good meal, and enjoy it to the full with none of the qualms of the would-be aesthete. Of course, during the day a Florentine cat may well drop into the Uffizi to have a look round, quietly slipping through the turnstiles without paying. But it will have an eye on the main chance while there are elevenses to be had at the Café Procacci, where my colleague Elizabeth David tells us they do a very nice mid-morning snack of white truffle sandwiches served with a glass of good white Tuscan wine. Perhaps after a couple of hours back in the galleries of the Uffizi, a light luncheon in Harry's Bar, with tea at Doney's and, if the cat is lucky, dinner at Sabatini's.

Of course, some cats are deprived of these pleasures. The cat brought up in an avant-garde household in Hampstead, for instance, whose owners have gone down to the Institute of Contemporary Art for the day, leaving it to prowl round the Habitat furniture and the David Hockney reproductions. As the day wears on, it begins to build up a feeling of resentful envy towards its Italian cousins, but decides this is not of much practical use and that it would be better employed in having a look round the kitchen.

There is a roll of kitchen paper made from recycled material by the Friends of the Earth, but as the cat's owners are strict North West Three vegetarians, there is not much else.

However, if they are not vegan vegetarians, at least there should be eggs, and hopefully some frozen spinach and cheese. From the deep-freeze the cat should take a packet of the spinach, preferably the chopped variety rather than the leaf, and thaw it out in a pan on the stove. When the stuff is de-iced, the cat should tip it into a small, shallow, buttered, oblong casserole, seasoning it before making three or four shallow dents in the spinach. Into each of these it should crack a free-range egg preferably obtained from a health food shop with vegetarian affiliations. My recipe says it should top all this with some anchovy fillets, but this kind of Hampstead household doesn't stock anchovies, being not only vegetarian but ecological to the point of neurosis when it comes to utilising the ocean's resources.

However, a cheese sauce made along the lines of a bechamel is a substitute, topped with more cheese and breadcrumbs, and fifteen minutes in a medium oven should see the eggs set.

It isn't what the cat would get in Sabatini's, but it is a Florentine dish of sorts and I used to eat it in the Kardomah in the King's Road years ago when I had no money for anything else.

VEGETABLE DISHES

 POIREAUX MORNAY

Unlike most dogs, a cat can play its cards remarkably well in the matter of dual residence. Displaying skills normally reserved for a practised bigamist, the cat can keep up two homes without attracting much comment or the attentions of the police, and my Welsh friend Blodwen showed a mastery of technique in the matter.

Blodwen ("Blodders" to her intimates) was the hotel cat at The Twelve Dogs Inn, but often she was not in residence, for when she became tired of hotel food she would quietly leave her habitual post by the refrigerator door in the kitchen and disappear for months at a stretch.

When she reappeared, rather like the Cheshire cat in *Alice in Wonderland*, we knew from her sleek, well-fed appearance that far from living rough, she had spent her absence in some hospitable hill farmhouse where a good table was kept, conning the owners into thinking she was "their " cat, just as she would now con the proprietress of The Twelve Dogs into thinking she was "hers".

In a sense it constituted a classic case of having one's cake and eating it, except that Blodwen, like most cats, didn't like cakes except for cream buns.

So I suggest that if you have an unexpected visitor from the Welsh principality drop in on your house, you offer it something savoury. Sewin (or salmon), coracle-caught in the swirling waters of the River Teifi, will go down well, but it is expensive nowadays and you may prefer to give the animal its national emblem, the leek, cooked in the style we gastronomic experts call 'mornay', that is in a creamy cheese sauce.

Most recipes recommend washing leeks before cooking them, but having an Irish friend who has convinced me that germs are good for the stomach, I just buy the cleanest-looking ones I can find and hope for the best.

But at least top and tail them before you fling them into the boiling salted water where they must stay for 10 - 15 minutes depending on their thickness. Then drain them and pour over the cheese sauce you have made in the meantime. This is simply a bechamel enriched with grated cheese and perhaps a little cream.

Over the top of the dish pour some breadcrumbs and more grated cheese and brown it under a hot grill.

When the cat has finished with the sauce, you will have some cooked leeks which you can use as a starting point for a number of other recipes for yourself.

ROUND AND ROUND THE CORNFIELD

Through the 1960s, I ran, every summer, a repertory company in a pleasant small seaside town, and come each July the whole family emigrated there to a house which we rented for the season.

Our cats, unlike some, never had any objection to travel. The head cat sat on my shoulder, acting as navigator while I drove, and the others studied the landscape through the windows of the car.

The first time we took them to the sea, the head cat went missing within a matter of minutes. This caused great anxiety to my wife, who went off in search of her and came back in half an hour to say she had found the animal playing happily on the beach and perfectly in control of its new surroundings.

It was the return journey that caused the trouble. They would wait until the car was packed and then dart across the road and hide in other people's gardens.

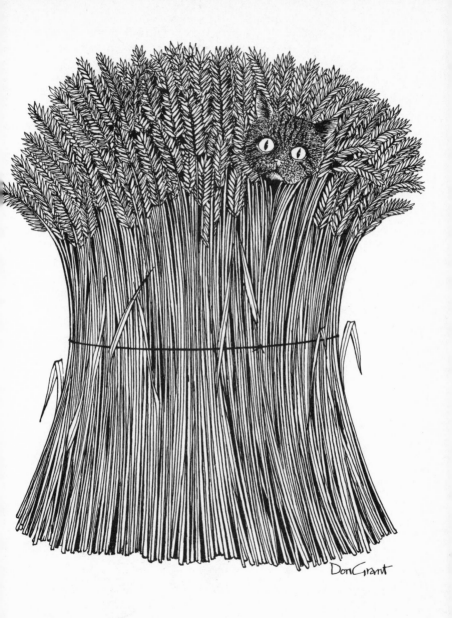

DonGrant

One got stuck up a tree and refused to come down because it was too fat from all the fresh local fish it had eaten during the holiday.

When we finally rounded all three up, the fat one, who was the head cat's elder son, caused further trouble by suddenly jumping out of the back window of the moving car, and disregarding the fast-moving stream of cars in the opposite traffic lane, somehow wove his way between their wheels to disappear into a cornfield from which it took us two anxious hours to dislocate him.

When we got home, I decided to put him on a punishment diet, and after racking my brain chose the corn dish. It was an invention of my wife's, and something to which she always resorted when we had no money for something better. I never liked it much.

It was based on a mixture of tinned sweetcorn, a seeded and cored green pepper cut in bits, a tin of tomatoes and a packet of frankfurters, everything being mixed up in a casserole and baked in a hot oven for 25 - 30 minutes. By subtracting the frankfurters, I could ensure that there was nothing of any interest for the cat, and once it saw the connection it stopped escaping into cornfields once and for all.

DIETING FOR CATS

WEIGHT-WATCHING FOR CATS

One of the hardest things is to get a cat to go on a strict dietary regime of its own accord, but our solution to the problem came unexpectedly through a Haitian voodoo priestess of our acquaintance.

The lady was our house guest at the time, and the popular daily press, getting wind of the event, arrived one morning in their droves to interview and photograph her.

One of them thought it would be a good idea to include the cat in his pictures. The animal was sought out and appeared to give its consent. But when the voodoo priestess, lying on a pink chaise-longue in the garden, took it into her arms, what had hitherto been a mild-mannered pedigree Abyssinian cat, now reverted to a savage, spitting creature from the wild.

Not only did it spit, but it snarled, revealing a number of sharp teeth which no-one but its dentist had seen before. Any normal person would have put it down at once. But not the voodoo priestess. The photographers moved in *en bloc*, their flashing cameras enraging the beast still further and providing some spectacular shots for their newspapers the following morning.

The ordeal over, the cat retreated angrily into the house, where it took up residence at the back of the wardrobe and refused to come out or speak to anyone about anything.

The voodoo priestess promptly made two acts of contrition. Firstly she spent the rest of the afternoon in the kitchen, preparing a very hot spiced Haitian meat dish, the ingredients of which I unfortunately did not record. Secondly she announced her intention of

51

making me "'er 'usband" that night.

The cat refused to eat the dish, but later my wife and I did, between copious draughts of cold lager and incessant choking fits. Afterwards we retired to bed. I was not then into polygamy, and my wife, protective of her marital rights, piled all the bedroom furniture against the door as there was no lock on it. The night passed without incident. I remained my wife's "'usband", and the only strange thing was that the cat stayed at the back of the wardrobe and continued to refuse all offers of food or conversation.

This continued for the next four days, after which the voodoo priestess left us for a furnished apartment» near Harrods. As the taxi sped away from the door, the cat emerged from its hiding place, noticeably slimmer but smiling quietly, and resumed its normal eating habits.

Unfortunately I am unable to advise you where to get hold of a voodoo priestess, as although ours was heard of ten years ago in a Paris night-club, she has since disappeared without trace and I haven't come across another one.

 CUISINE MINCEUR FOR CATS

There was a time when I could have told you what the cat and I were having for luncheon or dinner on, say, Friday week. Most cats still can: a saucer of milk, half a tin of Kit-e-Kat or Happy Pet (Happy Pet is particularly suitable for Fridays, being 100% fish of South

African origin) and, if they are lucky, a vitamin pill by way of apology for their not being fed a more interesting diet.

It was Monsieur Michel Guérard of cuisine minceur fame who drew my attention to menu-planning. Monsieur Guérard says you should draw up your menus in advance, a week at a time, and you must stick to them without deviation.

For instance, on Tuesday, luncheon comprises a mousseline of frogs' legs with watercress, followed by a leg of lamb cooked in hay and a pudding called floating islands with blackcurrant sauce. The mousseline was easy — I did it with the asparagus sauce listed as No 63 of Monsieur Guérard's recipes — but I had to cook the lamb without hay, as London's last hay market was discontinued in 1927. The same thing happened that night over dinner, which called for a soup of vineyard thrushes, but though there is now a greater acreage of vines under cultivation in England than at any time since the Middle Ages, their owners simply wouldn't let me come and shoot their thrushes.

Wednesday was easier, luncheon starting with a pigeon salad with chervil and going on to chicken served in a soup bowl with crayfish. This is exactly how cats like to eat chicken. The soup bowl makes for easy pickings, and the tasty freshwater shellfish on the side give the dish an unexpected piquancy.

Of course, I was busy from first thing at dawn until we went to bed, but all went well for a few days, and we worked our way through many fine dishes appealing to the cat's palate: Iranian Sevruga caviar with creamed eggs for instance, a delicious starter to precede steamed calf's liver with leeks in a sweet-and-sour sauce. Lots of delicious fish like John Dory with Sabayon sauce and saffron-steamed turbot studded with anchovies, though we had to omit the sea bass cooked in seaweek, as seaweed is as difficult to find in London as hay is. But at least I managed veal kidneys in what Monsieur Guérard calls 'en habit vert' and his translator a green waistcoat; also a seafood pot-au-feu and a mushroom and sweetbread ragout which took me four hours to prepare.

This was Saturday luncheon's main course, and starting as soon as I got up from the table to prepare our simple dinner of lobster with a fresh tomato and basil sauce, I was a trifle generous to myself with the old Armagnac that Monsieur Guérard thriftily recommends for cooking purposes, and fell asleep over the stove.

I woke at drinks time and although the delay had put me back by several hours, I set to work again with a will, and in the moments I was unoccupied in chopping vegetables and pounding basil, devised several interesting new cocktails with the armagnac. I am not absolutely sure when I woke, but I think it must have been nearly midnight. The two ¾lb lobsters Monsieur Guérard specifies — one for each person — had somehow disappeared from the draining board where I had left them, and listening through the open kitchen window at the chorus of cats celebrating Saturday night on the next-door roof, I drew my own conclusions, which were that I didn't like being taken advantage of and that from now on I would feed the beast as and how I chose.

SOCIAL PASTIMES
for the
CAT-ABOUT-TOWN

 DINNER PARTIES FOR CATS

These things are really only supposed to take place in illustrated books for children, but I did once in real life arrange a dinner party for our cat. Whether Barbara Cartland or Emily Post would have acknowledged it as a social event is another matter.

The cat had been given to my wife and one day she told me that she had invited her mother — the cat's mother, not my mother-in-law — to dine with us that evening. It seemed that our cat's mother's owner was going out to the theatre and did not want her to be left on her own.

Even though it was I who, as always, did all the cooking, I raised no objection. I thought out a menu and made a seating plan. We ate in those days at a rather nice Georgian marble-topped table, but it was rather small for four people and in any case stood three feet off the ground, which is too high for small domestic cats. I therefore fetched a laundry box and put it on the floor with a place setting at each end: a bowl of water, a clean dish, but no utensils. Then I got on with the cooking.

About seven o'clock the doorbell rang and my wife admitted the visiting cat and its owner, a ballet dancer who though christened Diana was known universally as Pussy. As soon as Pussy had the creature settled in, she went off to her theatre.

Presently I announced that dinner was served and summoned the visitor to the table, where her daughter was already seated. I indicated that she should take the other end of the makeshift table. But instead of the

55

usual greetings between parent and offspring, and with a total lack of filial piety or even basic hospitality, the resident cat exploded in a fury of hissing and snarling, and letting out the most blood-curdling of screams, shot out of the window on to the roof, where she remained dinnerless for the next twenty-four hours, moodily contemplating the bright lights of Sloane Square and refusing all blandishments to rejoin the party. Her poor mother sat uncomfortably at the table, wondering what kind of manners her daughter had learnt in our household.

It was, as I firmly told her the following day, a disgraceful way for a cat to welcome a visiting relative in her own home, but the psychiatrist I went to see about it, said he thought the animal was expressing a resentment against her mother for parting with her at the age of six weeks and before she had been properly weaned.

CHARITY BEGINS AT HOME

Where I live in London is a great place for jumble sales. A week seldom goes by without several of these taking place, but as I am not much interested in old hats and broken electrical appliances, I usually only drop by to see if there is any food going.

Old food doesn't sound interesting either, and isn't, when it takes the form of rusty tins of processed peas and baked beans, or spaghetti rings and sultana puddings. Cats don't like them.

But we also have some rather up-market jumble sales, which are not called jumble sales but Christmas Markets, Spring Fayres and Autumn Bazaars. The best one in the Chelsea calendar is run by the ladies of the diplomatic corps in London who man stalls selling goods from the countries their husband represent.

MORE TABBYOCA PUDDING, MY DEAR?

They are new goods, not second-hand ones, and apart from the Indian shawls and the Czechoslovakian glassware and the Javanese dolls, there is quite an amount of food and drink on display. The drink is especially appealling because it obviously comes in through diplomatic channels and sells at less than the amount of the government tax that would otherwise be payable on it.

One day I was wandering about Chelsea Town Hall clutching a bottle of Brazilian fire-water that had cost me the price of two packets of cigarettes, when a voice came over the loud-speakers to say that caviar was now on sale on the Iranian stand. With a hungry animal at home to feed, I was there immediately, enquiring the price from the elegant Iranian ladies in charge. But not having bought the animal caviar for some time, I was not sure how favourable the price was, and making some excuse about fetching my cheque-book, I asked the ladies to keep me six tins of the stuff and made for the nearest telephone.

The target of my call was Harrods, where the tame Jeeves in charge of the caviar department suavely quoted a price six times what the Iranian ladies were asking for a tin of much the same size and quality. Bertie Wooster thanked Jeeves for the information and said he would be round later.

Instead of which, he returned to the Iranian ladies, gave them a cheque for his six tins, six for the price of one, so to speak, and made for the nearest exit and the cat.

Unfortunately we haven't had the delicious substance since, because the present incumbents of the Iranian Embassy in London seem less disposed toward the charitable work performed by their predecessors, and at least one Persian cat feels badly let down by the Ayatollah Khomenei.

No-one has lived until they have been shopping for and, preferably with, a cat, but even I, who have done some fairly offbeat things in my time, was thrown when my American publisher asked me to go to Harrods and buy £25 ($50) worth of groceries for the animal, at his expense.

I should perhaps explain that when I talk grandly of my American publisher, I mean he is an English publisher who happens to be American, something no amount of residence in this city can erase, and he seems to think that my superficially patrician manner can intimidate the staff of Harrods in a way he can't.

So here I was, wanting to get on with my next book, but obligated to purchasing £25 worth of groceries suitable for a cat, and also to obtaining a Harrods Christmas hamper to put them in, so that my publisher could arrange some publicity display at the autumn Book Fair in Grosvenor House.

Abandoning the new book, I got out the car and drove the cat and myself to Harrods. The first thing I did was take the cat down to the kennels where customers are obliged to leave their dogs because, among other things, it is alleged that they upset the Arabs in Harrods.

The attendant, however, refused to accept the cat, saying that it would upset the dogs (not the other way round), so I tucked it under my right arm and made my way to the Food Hall.

I had been instructed by my publisher to see one of the gentlemen in charge. He was not available in person, but I was allowed to speak to him on the house telephone, holding the receiver with my left hand while I balanced the cat with my right.

"Cuisine for Cats?" he said anxiously. "Well, you see we don't sell cat food in the Food Halls, but actually quite a lot of people can't be bothered to climb the

59

stairs to the Pet Department, so they buy things down here. Chicken fillets in tins, for example. No bones you see. Tinned pilchards are another favourite."

"We shall want a Christmas hamper to put them in," I said.

"Ah," said Harrods' man, his voice audibly changing gear, "May I just interrupt a moment. That comes under the Public Relations Department. If I may just transfer you."

It was still the voice of Jeeves, but there was a hard edge to it.

"Would you transfer this call to Public Relations," it said to the switchboard girl.

Nothing happened. Jeeves explained that the Public Relations Department's lines were always busy on Fridays, then said I could have the use of a phone to try myself, and gave me a number to ring.

I tried it for twenty minutes, during which people elsewhere were presumably saying that the Food Halls' lines were always busy on Fridays, then growing bored I decided to go out for a drink.

Still holding the cat in my right arm, I crossed the Brompton Road to a nearby wine bar, where I ordered a glass of white wine and instantly found myself writing an extra new piece for the current opus. It is the one called 'O Sole Miaou'.

Cheered, I returned to Harrod's, passing the Wine & Spirit Department en route to the Food Halls. They were holding a free tasting of J & B Rare Whisky. I applied for a glass and asked if I could use their house telephone to call the Public Relations Department. After several people had been consulted, they said I could, and this time I got through. I explained what I wanted, and why.

"Are you the gentleman that called before?" they asked.

"Cuisine for Cats," I replied, hoping to parry the question.

"Are you selling it in Harrods?" they enquired.

"Of course," I said.

"Have we placed an order yet?"

"Well," I prevaricated, "The book isn't quite yet finished, but as soon as it leaves the binders . . ."

"There's nothing we can do," Public Relations said, "When it's on sale in the Book Department, et cetera."

There were a lot of et ceteras stated and I couldn't help feeling that they had doubts of it ever being on sale in the Book Department.

It was a hen-and-egg situation. I hung up and turned the most winning smile I could on the young lady who was dispensing the J & B Rare Whisky.

"Do you think I could have another?" I asked, trying to look as beaten and frustrated as I was.

"Only one per customer," she said primly, and removed my empty glass from me.

I sat motionless, wondering what to do next. My first inclination was to transfer my custom to Fortnum & Mason, but I had no account there and insufficient money on me to pay cash. Also I dreaded the same scene being re-enacted after I had made my way up the length of Knightsbridge and Picadilly, carrying a cat that was becoming increasingly heavy and bored.

I went back into the Food Halls and picked up a wire basket. This presented problems, because if you have one arm occupied by a cat and the other hand is holding a wire basket, you have no free hand with which to transfer purchases from the shelves into the wire basket. I solved it eventually by putting the cat in the wire basket and piling the goods round and on top of it.

It is a myth that cats only like fish, but journalists like the extremely obvious and I wasn't going to disappoint the ones who would be coming to Grosvenor House. I chose several kinds of lumpfish caviar in glass jars, also a jar of salmon eggs for the colour contrast they made; tinned salmon, vintage sardines, mackerel, trout, a pack of four different tins of fish pâtés made in New Zealand, and a tin of condensed milk.

61

I was fortunate enough not to meet any of my friends as I usually do in Harrods. Often they hide behind the tall plants near the Fruit Juice Bar and jump out to say something witty and apt for the occasion like "Boo!" I could just see them peering into my wire basket of tinned fish while I explained that I was shopping for the cat.

I walked back to the car with the thongs of Harrods heavy Food Hall bag cutting into my left hand and prayed successfully that the bottom wouldn't fall out and scatter all the tins over Pont Street. It would have been a fitting climax to an unusual shopping expedition.

Audio-Visual Cat   Cat with normal sight and hearing.

Bain Marie   Bath Mary

Catfish   Also currently known as rock salmon for catering purposes.

Dogfish   Fish used for laboratory dissection purposes.

Flake   Government-approved term for rock salmon.

Fritto Misto di Mare   Italian restaurant term meaning fried sea mist.

Fumet   A fish stock used for making soups and sauces. Not to be confused with the French for 'Gentlemen, you may now smoke'.

Huss   See Flake

Langues de Chat   Cat with its tongue in its cheek.

Rigg   See Huss

Rock Eel   See Rigg

Rock Salmon

Dogfish eaten in fish-and-chip shops, but usage of term shortly to be frowned on by government regulations concerning the nomenclature of fish.

Seafood

Inflationary word for fish, esp. frozen shellfish.

Seafood Bar

Fish-and chip shop with ideas above its station.

Seafood Cocktail

Frozen prawns served in a pink 'cocktail' sauce which is caterer's mayonnaise coloured with bottled tomato ketchup. The ideal beginning to a cat's meal when it is dining out in a steak house. The frozen whitebait makes a good second course.

Zabaglione

An Italian pudding combining egg yolks, sugar and marsala wine. May well appeal to a cat with a sweet tooth and alcoholic disposition. Try serving it with double cream.

Zafferano

Italian for saffron. Used in rice dishes as well as in some fish soups. Author estimates that the little packets of it sold in Harrods work out at the equivalent of around £300 per lb.